My dad

by Jenny Giles
Photography by Bill Thomas

Here I am with my dad.

My dad is very big,
and I am little.

Dad's shoes are big,
and my shoes are little.

Dad's hat is big,
and my hat is little.

On sunny days,
we all go down to the beach.

I sit way up
on Dad's shoulders.

I go into the water
with Dad.

I play in the waves,
and Dad looks after me.

Dad is good at cooking.

He cooks hot dogs
for Mom and me.

Dad likes painting.

I look after Dad.
I get him a drink.

I like painting, too.

Dad helps me
paint a sign
for my playhouse.

I help my dad,
and my dad helps me.